THE APRICOT
AND THE MOON

POEMS BY

CATHRYN ESSINGER

DOS MADRES

2020

DOS MADRES PRESS INC.

P.O. Box 294, Loveland, Ohio 45140
www.dosmadres.com   editor@dosmadres.com

Dos Madres is dedicated to the belief that the small press is essential to the vitality of contemporary literature as a carrier of the new voice, as well as the older, sometimes forgotten voices of the past. And in an ever more virtual world, to the creation of fine books pleasing to the eye and hand.

Dos Madres is named in honor of Vera Murphy and Libbie Hughes, the "Dos Madres" whose contributions have made this press possible.

Dos Madres Press, Inc. is an Ohio Not For Profit Corporation and a 501 (c) (3) qualified public charity. Contributions are tax deductible.

Executive Editor: Robert J. Murphy

Illustration & Book Design: Elizabeth H. Murphy
www.illusionstudios.net

Typeset in Adobe Garamond Pro, Copasetic & Skia
ISBN 978-1-948017-78-7
Library of Congress Control Number: 2020935192

ACKNOWLEDGEMENTS

I am grateful to the editors of the following publications in which these poems first appeared, some in slightly different forms:

Adelaide, "Anniversary," "On the Stairway," "How Words
    Become Things"
Alaska Quarterly Review, "Summer Apples"
American Life in Poetry, "Summer Apples," (reprint)
The Antioch Review, "For the Birds"
Blue Heron Review, "What He Saw"
Buddhist Poetry Review, "Another Stilled Thing,"
    "Something Always Happens"
Conrad's Corner, WYSO, "Enroute to Osaka," "Boo,"
    "Of Course...," "Cooking Soba in Ohio"
Dayton Metro Library Award, "Locking the Door"
Ellipses, "Alas," "Enroute to Osaka"
Every River on Earth: Writing from Appalachian Ohio,
    "Someday the Sycamores," "Beside Spring Creek,"
    "A Corner of the Moon"
Gnarled Oak, "Super Moon"
Innisfree Poetry Journal, "Away," "Zinnias"
Literature Today, "The Apricot and the Moon,"
    "The Carving Ritual"
Mad River Review, "Secret," "Of Course..."
Mock Turtle, "Three Mastiffs," "Halloween,"
    "After Flushing His First Muskrat"
Nimrod, "Deconstructing the Moon"
Panoplyzine, "Heliotrope"

Poetry Daily, "Missing Wakayama," (reprint)
The Southern Review, "Envy," Spring," "Why I Lifted the
        Moth from the Spider's Web," first published as
        "Missing Wakayma"
Tampa Review, "Reading Basho by Fernlight"
The Valparaiso Poetry Review, "October in the Workshop,"
        "All Hallows"
Waypoints, "Now and Again..."

This book is dedicated to the Moon,
our closest neighbor and most steadfast friend.

This collection owes a special thank you to the Greenville Poets:
David Lee Garrison, Suzanne Kelly-Garrison, Aimee Noel,
Belinda Rismiller, Lianne Spidel, and Myrna Stone.
Without their friendship, generosity, and expertise,
this book would not be possible.

TABLE OF CONTENTS

Π°Ш, ᴀɴᴅ AGAIN

THE APRICOT
AND THE MOON

ENVY

The moon climbs
until she can see
into every attic window.

SHE SAID THE WORD MOON...

For the Birds

At the farmer's market the grocer has decided
to give me a Bible lesson as I fumble for my wallet
to purchase a squash.

This one is called the Crown of Thorns, he says,
to remind us of the cross, and here are ten spokes,
one for each of the commandments.

I give the grocer his money, but my sympathy is
with the squash, whose nature has been hijacked
by religion. It fills my palm

with its hefty promise and I suspect it of knowing
the true art of resurrection—seeds packed
into a sinewy cave,

where the pulp is so fragrant that time holds still.
When I split the ovum with a knife I reveal
a space so private

that I am embarrassed to have looked, flesh as pale
as the new moon, and an aroma so seminal
that it stains all thought.

With the sharp edge of a spoon, I scrape out the seeds,
and, holding the soft entrails in one hand,
throw it all to the birds.

Another Stilled Thing....

Tangled in the roots of the sycamore tree,
a goose egg, cold, spattered with mud,
abandoned.

I wash it in the creek, decide to carry
it home for the neighbor boy
who loves stilled things--

fossils, locust husks, and sea shells,
anything that might have been,
but now is not.

But how oddly I walk now
with a cold egg in my hand.
No sliding over

hollow logs, no clumsy tumble down
the creek bank, before the dog and I
wade to the other side.

We honor its fragility, as if it might be
reawakened. It is, after all, an egg,
once warm, some bird's

blueprint for the future now lodged
in my hand, and if someone
has to give

the universe a kick to get things started,
why not us? Why not now?
Or is this grand silence,

this question that no one cares to answer
nothing more than the egg
that does not hatch?

Deconstructing the Moon

She says "moon," and the word forms like a bubble,
hovering close to her lips. She thinks *lunar,*
luminous, and *round,* but those words do not appear.

She says the word "light," and the moon
moves across the patio, touches the table top,
smears the grass like a slow snail, before it silvers

the maple and climbs to the top of the pines,
where it breaks *like an egg yolk,* spilling color
down upon the tree, where it mixes with the odor

of the pines, and she thinks *dampness* and *dew,*
but she says nothing, and then the moon is gone.
She could have said, "cloud," thought *rain, haze,*

cumulous, but she did not, and then it was lost
behind a bank of evening clouds, and she could
not turn away, or it would become something else.

What He Saw...

She holds the moon between two fingers
like a pearl and then places it in the sky
between the church steeple
and the distant river,

and if she tips her head for
just a moment, rests her chin
in her cupped hands, she might
become Art Deco,

a billboard perhaps by Mukta,
but she stands, picks up the check
and moves to the door just as
the moon clears the steeple.

It continues to rise after she is gone,
papery and thin, finding other landscapes
to imitate, all the while making
it clear that it is what it is,

and nothing more, no more a part
of art than the girl who created
the moment. Still, he thinks
about a watercolor by Monet

and then a Van Gogh arbor painted
"by moonlight." But it is not
until he pushes his books away,
spreads his hands on the table

that the moon, that sweet conspirator,
bends over the table and he sees
the smooth china of her face,
reflected in his empty cup.

Alas....

Lying in bed at night, I think
about my bones—the fringe
of fingers and toes, the geography
of tarsals, the elegant sweep of tibia.

Fibula, like legs of a Renaissance chair,
the lace of vertebrae, the airy rib cage.
But at the skull I always stop, my own
face unimaginable without its flesh.

This is where I draw the line, the one
image I refused to let my children
bring into the house even in adolescent
rebellion. *No skulls*, I said. Tattoos

and rings, jewelry from the hardware store
perhaps, but *no skulls*, as if I might stave off
that "Alas, poor Yorick" moment? Tonight
I tap lightly around my eye sockets,

feel for that bump on the back of my head
that my mother said made me family.
No dental records needed here, the coroner
will say...still, it is not my good bones

that keep me awake at night, but the thought
of them without me. Impersonal skull,
please show me the blessings of anonymity--
how to be unknown among the unknowable.

All Hallows

The inflatable ghost my neighbor has placed
on his front lawn has already done his job.

He startled me once in the moonlight, and now
I am ready to be done with him.

His wiggly fingers, his vinyl hide are no more
frightening than a Sunoco sign.

He's not like the spider that drops beside my ear,
or the ominous creak of an empty chair.

But what do I know about the supernatural?
Maybe plastic and glitter can be just as haunted

as any Halloween cliché. And, I do remember
the young man who appeared on my doorstep

one October evening, his grand cape floating
behind him, lifting in an imperceptible breeze,

and the little witch who appeared from nowhere.
I mean, No. Where. A small child, dressed in black,

unaccompanied on a moonlit night, her confidence
in our generosity so casual, so cheeky, that we

gave her everything we had and would have
given more, except she left just as she came,

unnamed, unannounced, her only protection her
naiveté and our reluctance to question her.

By morning the ghost will be nothing but a puddle,
his plastic smirk buried in the grass,

a sad reminder that everything can be deflated
in the light of day, and now I regret having

wished him ill. Who am I to prick the illusion,
to name the shades that honor the night,

especially here, in November's first light, when
suddenly everything seems holy, cold and bare?

To Name the Moon

The black cat walks the length of each fallen branch
measuring the height of a tree struck by lightning.

She paces, one foot after the other, until she reaches
the top of the fallen tree, and then she turns in place,

a little pirouette, an *entrechat*, the way a tight rope
walker repositions before heading back to the safety

of the platform, each step delivered with the casual
concentration of one who knows the day will come

when she will need these tricks in the thin air
beneath some canopy, when her last life will depend

upon all of the steps she has taken on firm ground.
She doesn't waver, or even pretend for a moment

this is not urgent, life or death practice for the day
when she will climb higher than ever before,

her last life held firmly between her teeth. Her plan
is to arrive in heaven, alive and well, ready to barter

with whoever holds sway over black cats and fallen
trees, ready to argue for nine more chances to spit

 at feral dogs, tempt the thinnest of ledges, name
the August moon, and call all of her children home.

For Boo

Beware, gods of salmon and tuna,
keeper of mice and moonlit nights,
I am sending ahead my cat, Boo,
stalker of crickets, lover of old shoes.

Take care, god of the can opener,
guardian of cushions and weathered sills.
Make clear the midnight path for her.
Grant the passage black cats have earned.

Let there be catnip tucked into old socks
and saucers of store-bought cream.
Let her voice be heard, as it surely will,
with complaints that were never quelled.

But if there is thunder and the heavens
shake and threaten to fall down upon her,
and she longs for that place beneath
the stairs where she was safe from dogs

and toddlers and the veterinarian's pills,
let her return to me as a familiar,
a shade, a companion beside my door,
her voice too persistent to be ignored.

Super Moon

June 22, 2013

Because I don't want my neighbors to think
that I am doing nothing except watch the moon

rise between the maple and the evergreens,
I place a book in my lap, put on headphones,

inch my chair a few degrees north just
to keep the moon positioned cleanly over

our little slice of suburbia. Soon a neighbor
will join me, place his lawn chair next to mine.

He sits down and begins to whittle, slicing pale
curls from a hickory branch which pool

around his feet. After the man in the moon
clears the telephone lines, misses the maples,

my neighbor asks, *What are you listening to?*
Nothing, I reply. *Hmmmm...*he says,

Maybe you should learn to whittle?
Are you going to teach me? I ask.

Sure, he says, *you begin by looking
at the moon...*

A Corner of the Moon

Last night I saw my neighbor throw
one leg over a corner of the moon.

He must have ridden it like that,
cowboy style, all night long.

I didn't see him again until dawn,
when he came whistling up the street,

slapping moon dust from his jeans.
He must have slid down onto a rooftop,

the way a short man leaves a tall horse.
He tipped his hat, said *Morning, m'am,*

but the dog just stood there, straight
legged and still, the way she does

when she knows something that I do not.
I served him coffee in my best china cup,

watched him lift it to his weathered face,
saw the coffee eclipse the cup, rise

and then fall back again upon itself,
the way night overtakes the day,

smooth and deliberate, with no hint
of remorse or explanation. He talked

about the weather, the lack of rain,
what drought was doing to his garden,

but his eyes stopped me, from asking
what I wanted to know about moonlight

and darkness. He just drained the cup,
chucked the dog under her chin and

whispered into her dark ear, *That's just
the way things are…just the way they are.*

Missing Wakayama

for my son, in Nachi, Japan

Why I Lifted the Moth from the Spider's Web...

The web was old,
littered with debris,
and the spider was gone.

Spring

The petals are almost as beautiful
on the ground as they are in the tree.

First we look up; then we look down.

Envy

The moon climbs
until she can see
into every attic window.

Serendipity

I am carving a pumpkin for my friend Jane
in memory of her cat Lucky, gone
for several months now, although
he persists the way black cats do,

moving quick-silver in the October
twilight, tricking us into believing
that with moonlight and darkness
all things become possible.

Call it necessity if you like that
brought him to your door, limping,
half-blind, unless you call it Luck,
which might explain the outcome.

If he tricked Fate into dealing him
a better hand, a warm bed, and shots
of Redi-Whip in his bowl, then call
it Destiny because it is so predictable.

An unfortunate lands a lucky home—
isn't this the fateful contradiction,
the stuff of clichés, the happy-ever-after
that we are forbidden to write about?

So, please, accept this gift of the season,
knowing that it is bewitched with luck
and charmed by its own possibilities.
Trick or treat, Jane. Trick or treat?

TANGLED in TIME...

The Blue Heron, Fishing...

I named him
Heraclitus

because every day
he steps

into my stream
and every day

I follow in the wake
of his stepping,

just as nameless
as he was

before I named him.

Reading Basho by Fern Light

When the winter chrysanthemums go,
there's nothing to write about
but radishes.   —Basho

I am reading Basho, and the house
is so quiet my heartbeat paces itself
against the kitchen clock.

Tick and tock, we take turns spelling
hiragana until even the fern decides
to give it a try.

Hello, こんにちは she says, dipping a frond
to the turtle in the aquarium, to the dog
asleep on the rug.

Together we make the sign for green,
and wonder if anyone has noticed.
The violet seems attentive,

with that open face, simple blossom, as if
he did not know the season. The glare
from January snow

throbs against the window, and we sign
white, joy, happiness, lovely, きれい,
and her favorite—the sun!

And then we talk about the predictable—
the shade of afternoon, the dingy light
of evening

24

with just the saffron of an electric bulb,
sad imitation of the real thing.
And language, such a pitiful

translation of what we already know—
there is no substitute for the world itself,
for the immediacy

of sunlight, the nightly plunge into darkness
the motion of stars, the little grief
at the end of every day.

Heliotrope

The clock on the microwave agrees
with the clock on the stove,
which agrees with the clock on the mantle,

but I prefer the grandfather clock who always
lags a moment behind, the shadow
of the earth eclipsing the moon

above his numeraled face. He understands
that time is not some digital mystery,
but a slow grinding of the cosmic gears,

the turning of the earth measured against
its own circumference...25,000 miles around
its middle and still we say time flies.

Today my son is flying west, ahead of the sun,
arriving before he has left, his day
nothing but mid afternoon,

but now even the sunflowers in my garden
who followed the light so faithfully
from east to west are stilled,

preferring to wait for that blast of afternoon
light that pins them in place, causes
their heads to droop,

makes them long for earthly time,
the darkness of the soil, the steady
tick-tock of the sleeping seed.
.

Zinnias

for Becky,
1951-2017

Sometimes the answer forms around you
before you are aware of the question,

the way petals contract in a cool room,
or August nudges into September,

leaves looking a bit tired and out of sorts,
and then suddenly it is autumn, the time

for decision making gone, and you set off
on a new path, knowing that it is inevitable,

that the decision never included a choice,
you only pretend you had some control

over the spinning of the planet, or the way
sunlight slants across the floor in October,

reminiscent of summer mornings so full
of desire. Light christens the geraniums

you rescued from the cold, brought inside,
as if that might be a substitute for summer,

for the shortening days, the freeze that is coming,
if not tonight, then very soon. You will cut back

the zinnias and gather a few seeds to tuck away,
hoping to plant them in the spring, knowing

that you will forget where you saved them,
and they will slumber in a forgotten place

wanting to be zinnias, but stalled forever
in some empty space, neither here nor gone.

A Story:
Twelve Moments Tangled by Time

The clouds rush up over the hill
  with an urgency
I have never seen before.

The wind has a story to tell.
  I listen as if
it were meant for me.

In a circle of matted grass
  a young fawn
has come back from the future.

There is a deer stand
  among the sycamores
and corn spread in the meadow.

The corn brings a young buck
  up the creek bank,
into the silence of the morning.

If not for his head thrown back
  with such abandon
he might be asleep in a thicket.

The story tangles in the branches
  of the sycamores
still lost in the shadows.

A piece of bloody bone interests
    the dog more
than blackbirds flocking overhead.

I am more interested in blackbirds,
    whose calligraphy
I do not know how to read.

The creek eddies around a rock,
    water moving forward,
    backwards, all at the same time.

Nothing left but the hooves, ears,
    a bit of hide, the brain picked
from the small bowl of the skull.

From the tangled ridge line,
    I can still see the white
warning flash of his tail.

The Hourglass

for Myrna

This hourglass doesn't measure anything
without a little nudge to get it started.

The sands of time weren't meant to cling,
but this hourglass doesn't measure anything.

Memory does not honor time, but flings
its shade across any course you've charted.

This hourglass doesn't measure anything
without a little nudge to get it started.

So nudge the hourglass, get it started.
Memory does not change the course of time,

but parses this moment from the departed,
who nudge the hourglass to get it started.

Haunt the attics, let the ghosts be counted.
Memory cannot ignore this rhyme.

Just nudge the hourglass, get it started,
Memory does not change the course of time.

Secret

The eggs sit upright in the pan
like a covey of pigeons,
quivering slightly as the water
begins to boil, trembling with
their own self importance.

I did not ask the grocer
if the eggs were fresh, fertile.
It doesn't matter; it's their shape
that I am hungry for—fatter
than a droplet, firmer than a plum.

They tap against one another
jostling their need for space,
against my need to know,
and mimic a conversation
I barely hear. I watch the clock instead.

And now cold water, the easing
of the shell, the cup, the spoon,
and a question that I will not ask,
until you break the yolk, and spill
the silence we've coddled in this place.

On the Stairway

I.

He was coming up the stairs
as she was coming down,

and for just a moment his eyes
were level with her sandaled foot,

the painted nails, the pale arch.
He saw her toes lap gently over

the edge of the step, and then
her arch rose, and she continued

to move away from him. He never
saw her face; he didn't glance over

his shoulder to see where she was
going, and yet he never climbed

these stairs without remembering
the sparkle of a gold buckle,

a bracelet eclipsing the hollow
of her heel, and then she was gone.

II.

Odd how you can take such moments
with you--they ride along like shadows,

almost unseen. It wasn't anything--
it wasn't a kiss or even a smile.

Still he never mentioned it to his lover,
or to anyone for that matter. He kept

the moment to himself, a selfish pleasure
perhaps, but it was such a small thing.

And yet, he never climbed the stairway,
never let his eyes fall on that particular

place without remembering, without
thinking to himself, *How lovely.*

Away

I went away for awhile, she says,
and the stillness in her voice silences

the little café, and for just a moment
we all go with her. We drift away

from coffee, and notebooks, and Iphones
to wherever away is--that small space

that we promise ourselves,
that precious thing from childhood

within reach once again. It is the step
you take backwards before opening

a door, the calm just before sleep,
a moment to remember whoever

you truly are. And then in the clink
of a glass it is gone, and someone

is handing you a check, and you are
saying thank you, and finding change,

and you are back in the world...

But, deep in memory, there is a charm,
a talisman that knows you are never

really gone, that you are here and away
all at the same time. And for a moment

you are that child again clutching
your dolls in a photo less impressive

than a mother's desire to take it.
Sunburned children, cheeks smudged

with summer sweets, hair straggling
across our faces. In that moment

you remember that you were loved,
loved enough for a mother to take

a picture on an unremarkable summer
day when there didn't seem to be

an end to anything, much less to love.

Someday, the Sycamores...

...are going to pick up their roots
and walk away, but for now they are waiting
for the young ones to grow legs.

It is a slow, but inevitable process. Danger inches
closer every year. There is the creek, and the bank,
and, of course, the road

and the railing which keeps the road from tumbling
into the creek. Danger is slow but ever present,
and they are watchful.

Any season it might be necessary to raise the alarm.
Some will undoubtedly be left behind--the old,
the very young,

those who live so close to the edge that there is no hope
of their safe return. Still, the sun shines, they stretch
and grow, years pass.

Some fall in love with rocks and will not be budged;
others are in debt to the wind, but all worship
the sun that urges them upward,

all elbows and knees and crooked joints, climbing
some invisible ladder that gives them courage
to try the impossible.

When the ice melts, and the stream rushes forward,
undermining roots, lifting boulders like tombstones,
they know it is time.

And if you watch carefully, if you sit down in the dark
when the moon, that old tattletale, is out of sight,
you will see them stand

on gnarled knuckles and inch away, see them gather up
their children, hand in hand, and even if you call,
they will not turn back.

Beside Spring Creek

(Ohio River Valley Watershed)

The dog and I have sat so long beside the creek,
suspended between the reflected world
and the one above,

we can no longer tell the difference between
the shimmer of the water and the gleam
of a September sky.

The white sycamore branches thread their way
along the creek bottom where the dog hunts
the nether world,

neither here nor there, watching for crayfish stilled
by the autumn chill, or...yes...for a squirrel
that will make the leap

from one familiar limb to another. Trusting his own
lucky instincts, the dog plunges into the stream.
The water rocks

with the explosion, the sun rippling like a pennant.
But with no scent to follow, he gives up the chase,
returns to the bank,

wet, but not discouraged. It was not an illusion; he does
not feel tricked. It's simply the way things are--
like the face that I see

in the watery shadows, the hand on my shoulder,
warm and familiar, that causes me to look up,
even when there is no one there.

The Old Heron, Rising

Spring has arrived with the old clichés intact--
fragile and persistent, billing and cooing.

Beside the road, the bones of the little fox tangle
with new grass, and once again the creek gurgles

with snow melt; watercress blooms in the shallows.
The old heron who refuses to migrate, the one

I watched all winter, huddled beneath windbreaks,
standing in pools rimmed with ice, understands

that beginnings always foreshadow their ends.
Once again, he is preening his winter blues, checking

the skies for that first glimpse of a pretty wing tip,
enough to make his old heart rise and rise again.

And so he waits…loneliness still part of his intrigue.
Soon, there will be the release of summer, and for

a few days, in the cracking of the eggs, in the cries
of the young, there will be the bliss of belonging.

After Flushing His First Muskrat

Since he is a modern dog who expects kibble
in his bowl and a bed from LL Bean, I open
Wikipedia and read to him about muskrats—

"semi aquatic rodents familiar to most inland lakes
and streams," and he moves closer, panting
thoughtfully, so I continue. According to legend,

it was the muskrat who made the Earth, although
all of the other animals tried. It was only he who
could dive to the bottom of the primordial sea

and bring back enough mud (on his nose) to smear
on the turtle's back where the earth then took shape.
And the dog thinks this is possible—he has seen

muskrats dive, and it is impressive, and he has seen
their dens stacked beside the stream like small cottages.
It's the next part that worries him: "When the woman

fell from the sky, in her skirts were the seeds to grow
the trees, the corn, the grasses…." He has never seen
anyone fall from the sky, although he has watched

the woman stumble about at the edge of the stream,
crouching in the grass to return a turtle to the water,
and even bend over the fox, dead in the meadow,

42

to see if it could be brought back to life.
Mostly, he remembers the smell of wet musk in
his nostrils, the adrenaline rush as the animal

dove between his legs and slid into the current.
And then it was gone, leaving only the world that
he loves behind—the mud beneath his feet,

water pushing forward, the dizzying mix of sun
and shadow. Of course the story was true--
why would anyone doubt it? Just look around...

"Memory is the thing you forget with."

Alexander Chase

Two a.m. and the dog comes home redolent of skunk,
the odor preceding her, an appointment with dread.

We get out the peroxide, the baking soda and proceed
to wash her down until she smells more like a wet dog

than skunky musk, but as she dries, we're not so sure.
Months later, on a country road, I smell that pungency

again and relive details I never sought to remember--
barberry scratches on my ankles, the dog's sturdy

back under my gloved hands, the moon watching over
my shoulder as I whip suds from the dog's long tail.

Where does a memory reside when not remembered?
In the empty halter my brother carries home, proof

that he lost the dog on a midnight run, in the gloves
(my good gloves!) that I throw into the trash?

Or do memories hunker down along the river where
feral things roam, unnamed, until we recreate them

from the slap of the waves, the throb of locusts,
or from a wet dog shivering under a soapy moon.

44

Unwatched

The small brown bird that hit
the window early this morning
lay dumbstruck in the grass.
He raised his head, tried a wing,

decided to stay put, while I kept
an eye on the neighbor's cat.
Too tame to hunt, she is
nonetheless an opportunist.

And then I looked away for no reason
except to check the time of day.
(Was it early or was it late?)
When I turned back, both were gone—

no fluttering in the leaves, no Blue Jay
calls, nothing to help me decide,
only this empty print in the grass
where he had lain all morning.

Isn't that the way it always is?
The thing you want to see most
eluding you, moving just
ahead of your expectations,

like a pinch of mercury, salt on
the tail of memory. Still, I know,
small things rise everyday and fly,
unwatched, into the teeth of it all.

Gossip

The crab trees grouped beside the road,
low and rangy here in November,
look as if they might break into a slow trot.

A group of yearlings, testing the first snow,
they huddle, break apart, gather again,
depending upon where you stand,

always keeping that discreet distance
that nature understands--close, but not offensive.
Only when the weather gets mean

will they huddle in the moonlight, rub snow
off each others' flanks with their noses,
let fog swallow their soft breath.

But when they gather beside the creek,
they whisper secrets so familiar
that no one needs to listen in order

to repeat the news to the sycamores,
to the choke cherry, to the pines.
(There are rabbits in the hedgerow,

a hunter crouches in the meadow,
a buck lies dead in the thicket.)
The pines repeat it to the sparrows,

and the sparrows carry it everywhere,
into the fields, across the highway,
into the housing development where

they nest in the eaves, and sometimes
early in the morning, when there is still water
in the gutters and before traffic has begun,

they repeat it in a language that even I
can understand—*Everything will be
different today, but nothing has changed.*

What the Wind Wants to Know

Wind comes rushing in from Oklahoma…Kansas…
Tennessee, beating on the house,
asking the old questions.

Why clouds, why rain, why this rushing,
this wringing of hands?
Why cat tails and stars?

Why tides, why the secrecy of the moon,
the cracking of the willow,
the terror of midnight?

And the house groans and tries to answer,
because it has no choice,
because it stands

where it has always stood, and the wind asks
the oak and the barn, and the silo,
and when no one answers,

she throws trash into the street, lifts shingles
and bullies the dog, who hunkers
down inside his shed.

Wind rips leaves from the trees, throws
them against the windows, where
they cling like hands,

like someone losing his grip, praying for
for morning, hoping that daylight,
although she has no answers,

will at least make the wind stop asking,
Where are we going? Why are we
always the last to know?

Locking the Door

The door is heavy, old, handmade, and it has many locks.
There is a deadbolt to keep out people, a sliding bar
to lock out the night, and wooden levers, top and bottom.
But tonight, there is nothing to keep out except hemlocks

and ferns, the fawn we saw sleeping in the grass. But now
the door will not lock--the wood is not swollen,
the frame is intact. There is nothing to keep the door
from closing, except our desire to close it.

We stand in the kitchen, barefoot, pondering the problem.
The mountain must have moved, Jane says, and so we go
out onto the porch to watch the planet spinning on its axis,
the moon thrown up like a jump shot, the stream muttering

her usual discontents, and the mountain itself breathing,
a movement so slow and predictable, so tethered to the night
that we have forgotten for a moment that we are merely
passengers, three women who have come along for the ride

on a summer night when even locusts have decided to listen.
And we wait for the mountain to stretch, to yawn, to gather
the moon back into her arms, before we wake the dog,
step inside, and slide the locks back into place.

Blessing

The rabbit with the loppy leg is skittering
across the lawn, zigging when he should zag,

darting for the safety of the hemlock thicket.
I rein the dog in, wonder if the rabbit has a story

to tell, or if this lumpy gait is what he was born
with, all he knows about rabbit motion.

I saw the hawk in the Crab tree this morning.
She has a nest across the field, where fledglings

are whistling for their breakfast. I wish them all
a generous summer, the wistful grace of fall;

but when winter comes, let it be quick and clean--
not this limping toward hunger, no whistle of despair.

NoW, and AGAIN

Summer Apples

I planted an apple tree in memory
of my mother, who is not gone,

but whose memory has become
so transparent that she remembers

slicing apples with her grandmother
(yellow apples; blue bowl) better than

the fruit that I hand her today. Still,
she polishes the surface with her thumb,

holds it to the light and says with no
hesitation, *Oh, Yellow Transparent...*

they're so fragile, you can almost see
to the core. She no longer remembers how

to roll the crust, sweeten the sauce, but
her desire is clear—it is pie that she wants.

And so, I slice as close as I dare to the core--
to that little cathedral to memory--where

the seeds remember everything they need
to know to become yellow and transparent.

Now, and Again

Odd, how the old shoelace holds
frayed now to a single thread,
a few strands still caught in the eyelet,

even though I have twice bought
replacements, once because prudence
seemed to demand it, and again because

I lost the pair bought for prudence.
I should remove the old lace, but it has
become a curiosity, like the T-shirt

Mother laundered until it was thin
as cheesecloth. When she pinned it
to the line, I could see right through

to another time, to a landscape gauzy
through cotton mesh, where the Iowa
cornfields lie smothered in summer heat.

And I know now that time can be
caught in the thinnest of nets.
On laundry days, Mother would lick

her finger before tapping the hot iron,
the sizzle on the plate almost as reassuring
as the odor of ironed cotton. Never mind,

time will make us laugh about the days
when she ironed and starched her sheets.
Today, I remember the kittens who paced

the rim of the old washer, and when one
tumbles in, it is still her arm, soapy
and determined, that grabs the kitten

by the scruff of its neck. She holds it up,
half drowned, still dripping with suds,
and her words thread the memory into place.

Look at you…just look at you now!

The Apricot and the Moon

Solar Eclipse, 2017

We set a grapefruit in the middle of the table,
followed by an orange and an apricot,

and then we set both to spinning to show
how something small can eclipse the view

of something much larger than itself.
It all depends upon where you are standing.

(But now your father passes through to remind
us that the table and the room should also be

spinning at some rate still unknown even to
astrophysicists, but we decide to ignore him.)

You hold the apricot up to your eye and say,
Now I can see only part of the window,

and now I can't see the cat (who has come
to bat at the orange) *or any part of the clock,*

which makes telling time a problem, here at
the edge of our galaxy where such things matter.

And so you persist all evening, listing the things
you cannot see, until I put you to bed saying,

Now, I can't see the moon, and I can't see you.
You fall asleep with the apricot on your pillow.

I am afraid for you, until I remember that you
have an apricot to protect you from the things

you do not want to see. And I wonder if you
are right, if it is really that easy, so I get up

and look at the moon and extend my hand
until I cannot see that simple light.

How Words Become Things

For June Belle

My granddaughter, not yet two, points at the moon,
and pipes along the length of her outstretched arm
the word, "*Balloon!*"

Charmed by her misconception, I correct her
nonetheless, saying. "*No, that's the moon,*" but
she just laughs,

placing her hand over my mouth and repeating,
"*Balloon!*" until she is sure I get the joke.
Already she knows

that every metaphor is a lie, and that language
alone will never suffice, no matter how words
rub against the things

they want to become, no matter how much static
they create or how many sparks rise
into the waiting air,

some things will always remain unnamed despite
our efforts to put words into her mouth.
It is not language

that causes her eyes to come open at night, or words
that pull her into my arms when owls hoot
their spooky syllables.

Words cannot find the silky blanket that has slipped
beneath the bed, or cause her head to drop
 upon my shoulder.

Still, lying in bed at night, I hear her practicing
her words, burbles that linger in the air...*yes,
like balloons...*

that float above her bed, soft and meaningless,
sounds that mean nothing,
nudging her into sleep.

Of Course...

for Levin

We hold the sonogram up to the light where
it resembles the map of an unknown country,

grainy, mountainous, its geography
still unformed, a landscape in progress,

and then we see, *of course*, the bony knob
of an ankle, the Mickey Mouse fingers,

and then a face so familiar that I know
I have seen you in another life.

Little traveler, you have set some clock
to ticking, and I will come to meet you

from a place not so far away. But for now,
I would not hurry this bliss, this sleep that

we cannot imagine. Still, I admit, there is
a wonder, a feeling of oneness that tells me

you are complete, even now before your eyes
have opened, before your mouth has found

your thumb. And when you are my age,
with the texture of a full life behind you,

remember me, please. Remember that I knew
you in this picture before I knew your name.

Cooking Soba in Ohio

In this familiar kitchen, steam
from soba noodles misting the air,
I practice my depth perception,
as the sun rises over my shoulder,

stretching the length of the crabtree,
the maple, the fence, and beyond it
the pines, the horse barn, the town
all growing smaller as if through

the far end of a telescope, until
the horizon bends and the sun
sets, and I follow it past plains,
coastal waters, oceans, and then

to a small town half way around
the world, and now I'm in the street,
looking for you, *watashi no musuko*,
here in the evening's dusk, reading

another alphabet, past markets
advertising moshi and American jeans.
I find you sitting in the glow
of a computer screen, a bowl

of soba noodles still steaming
in your hand, and you look up,
a bit surprised to see *me,*
of course, but never the soba!

Enroute to Osaka...

My son is asleep in a foreign land, his long limbs
lying diagonally across some hotel bed.

He has kicked off his shoes, but is still wearing
the tattered jeans I took from the dryer 24 hours ago.

Too tired to dress for bed, he sleeps in his traveling
clothes—American T-shirt and blue bandana.

He sleeps through our morning and all afternoon,
wakes as we reach for the lights, set the supper table.

Soon dawn will nudge him on his way, cause him
to rise, collect his bags and move on, *hikouki*

to *densha* to *basu*, he puts more miles between us.
But for the moment, in this nether time, neither

dawn nor dusk, the moon not waxing or waning,
while even the sun hangs indecisive, he is here.

Soon he will whistle for a cab, throw his pack
into the back seat and pick up his headphones.

Tomorrow, he will put on a *jinbie*, place his hands
together in thanks and explain to students

half a world away that somewhere in Ohio his family,
Watashi no kazoku, is preparing for the night.

Konban wa! he will say, *Ohayou gozaimasu* they will reply, as I turn off the lights, tell him good night.

October, in the Workshop

My father is at the lathe, turning a rung
for a chair that once belonged to his mother.

It has been broken as long as I can remember,
and my grandmother has been dead for 30 years.

I am doing it, he says, *because I promised her
that it would get done, and besides, I may be*

*the only person who remembers how it happened,
or who knows how to fix a worthless chair.*

He is the diligent son, the one she depended upon
to pick the cherries, mow the grass, mend the fences.

How did it happen, I ask, and he explains, *I imagine
my father used the rung of the chair as a ladder,*

and I am left to decide if this is possible, if a 300 lb
man would use a chair rung in this manner, or

if my father is looking for one more splintered thing
to lay on his father's grave, here, after all these years.

Outside the workshop, beyond the shadow of the house,
acorns are dropping so steadily they sound like rain,

geese are making ragged runs, modeling the V's
that will nudge them south toward warmer water,

and the sycamores are laying down leaves, one by one,
as if they were pages ripped from some angry book.

Dad pauses for a moment, listens with a drill
in hand, and then adds, *but maybe I'm being unfair...*

Anniversary

The Harvest Moon rising from
behind the strip mall appears tethered
to the horizon, but soon it will clear
the radio tower on the far side of town

and lift effortlessly past Walmart, Sunoco
and Payless Shoes. Pennants flapping
in the used car lot applaud the effort,
while tail lights flicker red in the exhaust.

He taps his wife on the shoulder and says,
Look at the moon, and she stands there
in the parking lot, hands pushed into
her coat pockets, shoulders hunkered

against the evening chill, while he loads
groceries and two-by-fours from Home Depot.
She is wearing her old coat with the frayed
collar over summer shorts and sandals.

There is a tenderness about her that makes
him want to pull her close, feel the cold lump
of her hand inside his own, but he just whistles
under his breath, *Shine on, shine on....*

She holds the grocery ticket in one hand,
meat and milk, and wonders how they came
to this moment, a middle aged couple,
children grown and on their own,

only the dog waiting for them in the house
that is almost paid for, and after all these years,
this moon still advertising, still outshining
anything that the world has to offer.

The Carving Ritual

Once again, my youngest son is carving a pumpkin,
sprawled on the kitchen floor, newspapers spread,
whistling to Nirvana on the stereo.

This is the child that I worry about, the one who
has yet to find his way, but for now he is carving
a wolf, a tree line, and a moon that will shine

its orange light across the neighborhood, regardless.
And there is an ache between my ribs that I might call
loneliness if I were alone, but is more of a hollow,

the absence of something, a want for someone else
that cannot be defined. Impossible to shape someone
else's vision, but for the moment, look at the wolf

with his nose pointed skyward, and the moon
that will come alive once we place a candle behind it.
Don't think about the forest, so dark and complicated,

think about the match and that moment when the lid
slips into place--the odor of ripened fruit, bruised
and warmed, will be ready to light the way.

Halloween

Halloween, a full moon, and my mother sits
with a basket of candy, asking again and again,
Are you sure that they're coming tonight?

Soon, all of the things that we have learned
to fear will show up at our doorstep. Children
dressed as the Grim Reaper, a ghost in tennis shoes,

my neighbor's 12 year old with a scythe over his
shoulder, his sister in a gypsy dress, a handful
of Tarot cards held out for us to examine.

Fate and death and the unavoidable have come
to beg for treats, and we hand them out--a quick
bargain made with the unknown, cheap at the price.

A Hershey bar to hold back the goblins of guilt
and sadness? So be it. Still, my father, impatient
as always, yells from the kitchen, *Tell them*

to stop ringing the damn bell, or we won't come!
We open the door anyway, hand out the treats,
welcome the tricks, and accept the inevitable.

Three Mastiffs

The neighbors' three mastiffs have come to visit,
so comfortable in their bigness
they see no need to hurry.

They come to look in our pockets, stand on our feet.
The puppy, already taller than the others,
studies my dad sitting on the step,

nose to nose—the perfect height for begging. Never mind
that it took Dad ten minutes to travel the length
of the drive, and now he must rest.

Big dogs know that the world moves at their speed,
and anything faster is panic, like the squirrels
that flatten themselves

beneath the hawk's shadow, or the deer that come to eat
the windfalls. They all scavenge for their treats,
but Jack Francis, Stella Moo,

and Hudson Mitchell depend upon pockets and store
bought chicken, "five buck clucks," to make
their suppers tasty.

Dependable friends depend on each others' generosity.
And why would the world not be generous?
It is October, and there are acorns

so thick it tests our balance to walk the lawn, and
walnuts drop like distant artillery. Nevertheless,
Hudson Mitchell wants his reward,

and there is no place better than an old man's pocket.
And the world, so weary with summer's excess,
opens her stores to provide.

Raking Leaves

for my father
on his 85th birthday

I know them each by the sound of the rake,
the shimmy of pine needles, the rustle of the oak,
the sycamores, heavy as parchment.
I know them each by the sound of the rake.

They mumble, gossip, whisper among themselves,
refusing to be rushed into forgetfulness.
Measuring the day against the stillness to come,
they mumble, gossip, whisper among themselves.

Remember us, they say, remember the faithful,
summer's abundance scooped and gathered,
heaped in front of the rake, final harvest of the year.
Remember us, they say, remember the faithful.

Time to repeat what the wind has taught--
why the sun will pick a single leaf to twirl,
autumn's clarity, the fickle nature of frost,
Time to repeat what the wind has taught.

I know them each by the sound of the rake.
They mumble, gossip, whisper among themselves.
Remember us, they say, remember the faithful.
Time to repeat what the wind has taught.

In October, We Count Our Losses

I go out in the evening's chill to cut
a handful of parsley and come in
with a caterpillar so large and hungry

that I set him in the middle of a bouquet
of parsley, dill, and rue, where he continues
to eat while we set the table, stir the soup.

Fifth instar, so late in the year, we list the things
he must have survived: September storms,
the starlings that stripped the garden,

drought, first frost--but now, suddenly,
this abundance, more than he can consume.
We talk about our losses as well--

people and places that cannot be reclaimed,
and how grief can become its own comfort,
even in the middle of the night.

By morning he has wandered away.
It will be a month before I find him
wrapped into a papery chrysalis,

plain and nondescript, a little mummy,
tucked on the underside of a chair,
where he will wait until spring, sheltering

on the porch while snow and rain pelt
the aging screens. Occasionally, I think
of him in his little ark, and the antifreeze

that he must have concocted in order
to survive this weather. About the time
I forget to worry if he will emerge

in the spring, I find him reborn, clinging
to the farthest screen, wings catching
the sunlight, warming to a new day.

There are so many of winter's little griefs
that I might bring with me into this Spring,
but I open the window, let them fly away.

About the Author

 CATHRYN ESSINGER lives in Troy, Ohio where she raises butterflies and tries to live up to her dog's expectations of her.

She is the author of three previous books of poetry- *A Desk in the Elephant House*, from Texas Tech University Press, *My Dog Does Not Read Plato*, and *What I Know About Innocence*, both from Main Street Rag. Her third book contains a video poem based on the way a community remembers a local murder. The video was produced by Cathryn's son, Dave Essinger.

Essinger's poems have appeared in a wide variety of journals, including *Poetry*, *The Southern Review*, *The New England Review*, *Rattle,* and *River Styx*. Her poems have been nominated for Pushcarts and "Best of the Net," featured on *The Writer's Almanac*, and reprinted in *American Life in Poetry*.

Currently, Essinger is a retired English Professor and a long standing member of the Greenville Poets.